# CONTENTS

# ABOUT THE AUTHOR

**DR. VALERIE SAXION** is one of America's most articulate champions of nutrition and spiritual healing. A twenty-year veteran of health science with a primary focus in Naturopathy, Valerie has a delightful communication style and charming demeanor that will open your heart, clear your mind, and uplift you to discover abundant natural health God's way.

As the co-founder of Valerie Saxion's Silver Creek Labs, a manufacturer and distributor of nutritional supplements and health products, Dr. Saxion has seen firsthand the power of God's remedies as the sick are healed and the lame walk.

Valerie is seen regularly on the weekly Trinity Broadcasting Network program *On Call* that airs worldwide on TBN, Sky Angel, Daystar, and the Health & Healing television networks. She has been interviewed on numerous radio talk shows as well as television appearances. Hosts love to open the line for callers to phone in their health concerns while Dr. Saxion gives on-the-air advice and instruction.

Dr. Saxion has also lectured at scores of health events nationwide and in Canada. After attending one of her lectures, you will leave empowered with the tools to live and love in a healthy body!

To schedule Dr. Saxion for a lecture or interview, please contact Joy at 1-800-493-1146, or fax 817-236-5411, or email at: valeriesaxon@cs.com.

Married to Jim Saxion for twenty-plus years, they are the parents of eight healthy children, ages 1 to 21.

# GETTING YOUR LIFE BACK

**SHE WALKED INTO** MY OFFICE FOR A consultation, and I immediately felt sorry for this 63-year-old female. Overweight and having all the telltale signs of being extremely tired and rundown, hers was a look I see everywhere I go. It's as though every ounce of what was once a vibrantly healthy life has been sapped, and there's little left but a quiet desperation to find hope that it can change.

In her hands was a cluster of medical papers and blood work that I knew represented an intense but unsuccessful search for a restoration of health. I took her paperwork and spent several minutes reading through a long list of ailments and symptoms. The more I read, the more I felt sorry for her.

Her problems included but were not limited to:

■ Elevated liver enzymes

- High blood pressure
- High cholesterol
- Low thyroid
- Significant fatigue
- All sorts of arthritic aches and pains
- Dry cough

While we talked, I discovered that she had been on numerous rounds of antibiotics for a variety of symptoms. And it was no surprise when she noted she was taking pain medications several times a day just to get through.

Truthfully, it took all of half a second after reading her information to determine that the first step she needed to take was a good detoxification program that included a serious liver and Candida cleanse. When I told her that, she was more than ready to try it although she was not familiar with the process. She was truly ready for change!

We sat down together, and I presented her with the same proven detoxification plan that is found in this booklet. She started the cleanse on a Friday and began with a three-day fast. You'll discover that although fasting means to not eat, it doesn't mean you should restrict yourself to water only. I encourage juice fasting, mineral drinks, as well as making green smoothies with our Creation's Bounty organic food supplement to make certain your body is not deprived of its needed nutrition.

She followed the simple plan, and from that day on she did not take any more pain medication. She also did the Candida cleanse for thirty days, and to her disbelief the weight literally fell off—she lost 30 pounds without even trying. (As you read through the booklet, you'll understand how cleansing out the Candida relates to weight loss.) When she went back to the doctor to get more blood work done, everything was in normal range!

Several months passed, and I was attending a conference of about 20,000 people. I went into the ladies room to wash my hands, and I heard someone say, "Hi, Dr. Val." I turned and did not recognize the face. It was the same 63-year-old woman, but she had lost 50 pounds and looked like a different person. It's hard to believe the change could be so drastic.

She was so excited that a few days later she brought her husband to the office to meet me. He thanked me for returning his wife to him. Now that she was so full of energy and looking so good again, he was trying to keep up with her.

# SO HOW ARE YOU FEELING?

**WHENEVER I AM** ON TELEVISION, or speaking at one of my seminars, or sitting on an airplane and the person next to me discovers I am a naturopathic doctor, the constant complaint I get is this: "It's been a long time since I really felt good. I'm tired all the time. I'm exhausted and rundown. How can I start to feel good again?" My response is, "Why don't you feel great all the time? Why are you willing to settle for feeling less than 100 percent?"

I am constantly amazed at how few people tell me they are living in great health. The long lists of complaints range the full gamut of maladies—high blood pressure, high cholesterol, constant fatigue, headaches, multiplied aches and pains, as well as fully developed diseases. Many spell out personal symptoms of diverse emotional problems, some of which have resulted in anger and frustration or feelings of hopelessness and depression.

People seem to assume that doctors carry magic pills that will suddenly transport them to the land of radiant health. Unfortunately, there are no magic vitamins or minerals or hormones that do the trick. If you are experiencing a decline in health or a specific health problem, it usually has come on gradually and perhaps has been nearly undetectable. What is happening is that your body is sending you a signal that your body cells are in dis-ease. You have stepped out of homeostasis, "the state of being in health." Those body cells are not receiving the nutrients they need to sustain or propagate healthy cells, tissues, and organs. Dis-ease is associated generally with the absence or lack of some substance from our system, and/or a buildup of toxins in the bowels that needs to be eliminated.

Our typical response to the onset of a symptom or disease is to run to our medical doctor to get fixed, but doctors' prescriptions are seldom the "silver bullet" that answers the real problem. Too often we have been doing and are doing things to our bodies that cause the problems, and if these are left unresolved, our problems will persist or get worse. Years of abuse bring us to these points, and a quick and easy fix won't mend what's broken. It usually takes a complete program to provide your body with all the nutrients, minerals, exercise, and other sources it needs in sufficient and balanced quantities.

You are mistaken if you think that you are in good health today because you are free from disease. Most of us hope we can defy the laws of nature when it comes to our high-fat or unbalanced diets. On top of that, relatively few of us exercise, and millions of Americans abuse tobacco and alcohol despite prolific warnings. "Do not be deceived," the apostle Paul wrote two thousand years ago, "God cannot be mocked. A man reaps what he sows" (Galatians 6:7). Your body may have been able to cope for a lack of a specific nutritional substance for a while, but you can only cheat for so long and not pay a price. We're simply reaping the harvest we sowed by failing to treat our bodies with the respect they are due.

Besides the harm we may be doing to our bodies through poor diet habits and lack of exercise, there are other factors constantly warring against us—not all of which we can control. The effects of breathing in smog and cigarette smoke, exposing our bodies to increasing levels of UV rays, and contact with chemical products as well as their fumes have shown to cause damage to the cells of our bodies. We are surrounded by pesticides, asbestos, formaldehyde (in particleboard, plywood, paints, and plastics), vinyl chloride, radioactivity, and X-rays—all of which are dangerous.

Add to that the preservatives and chemical additives to food, agricultural pesticides and hormone-enhancing drugs, chemical sprays, food processing, cured and processed meats, even our deodorants and shampoos, and the tremendous amounts of sugar added to our food. Government statistics state that the average American consumes a whopping 120 pounds of sugar each year, which is about 1/3 pound per day. Then there are the millions of daily stresses upon our lives that take their toll on our energies and health—emotional traumas of all sorts, physical injuries, crash diets and excessive exercising (to try to compensate for our lack of balance), allergies, antibiotics (that kill both bad and good bacteria in the body), and the fluctuations between hot and cold surroundings. All these negatively affect us over time, and one might think it a wonder that anyone is healthy.

There is good news, though, despite the bleak picture I've painted. Even if you have eaten badly since the day you were born and are suffering some bad effects in your body, God is a God of restoration. He has made your body in such a wonderful way that it is ceaselessly trying to make and keep you well. There is hope for every situation . . . even yours. At any moment, 50 percent of your cells are alive, 25 percent are dying off, and 25 percent are dead—this is a phenomenal process of regeneration. Your body is making billions of new cells right now. It is so efficient that if you are eating right, your liver regenerates itself every 7 days. It is actually possible to clean your body quickly and build health back into all your organs.

As long as those new body cells are being manufactured, you can make a difference in your health. These cells reach into your bloodstream to obtain more than 50 chemicals: amino acids (the building blocks of protein), fatty acids, minerals, trace elements, vitamins, and enzymes. These chemicals come from the food you eat, the water you drink, and the air you breathe—all of which you can do something about.

This booklet will teach you one of the most basic steps you can take to give your body the opportunity to start feeling great. Cleansing your body of impurities and renewing your body from within is simple, and it is wonder-working. It is totally doable, and you can start right where you are today.

Your attitude determines how great you can feel. If you want unbounded energy and an abundance of health in your everyday life, it begins with simple choices only you have the power to make.

# DETOXIFICATION

**DETOXIFICATION** IS A CLEANSING process that is going on inside your body every second of your life. If your body fails to eliminate its toxins daily, eventually you will die an earlier death than you should have. Our purpose here is to explore ways you can help this process that is so essential to rejuvenating the body and helping you feel great all the time. You can improve the quality of your life as well as the length of your life by following the suggestions of this booklet.

Fasting is one method of detoxification to which I devote a large section of this booklet. I consider it the most effective and practical and quickest way to cleanse your system. Yet I recognize that it is a more extreme form. There are many ways to detoxify, some of which we will consider here.

No one escapes toxins in this world. A toxin describes the chemicals in your body that have not been made harmless or "detoxed."

Toxicity occurs on two primary levels. First, toxins are taken in from our environment through the air we breathe, the food and water we consume, and through physical contact with them—environmental pollutants, food additives, and chemicals being the major ones. The majority of allergens and drugs and also mercury fillings in the teeth can create toxic elements in the body.

Second, your body produces toxins naturally all the time. Biochemical, cellular, and bodily activities generate waste substances that need to be eliminated. Free radicals, for instance, are biochemical toxins. When these are not removed, they can cause tissues and cells to become irritated or inflamed, blocking normal functions on a cellular, organ, and whole-body level. Yeasts, intestinal bacteria, foreign bacteria, and parasites produce metabolic waste products that we must process and eliminate from our bodies. Even stress creates a toxic state, if we allow it to dominate our mind and emotions.

Your body was designed by God to eliminate toxins, but over time these chemicals can build up in your system and overwhelm your ability to remove them. Or you yourself might be overpowering your system by the amount of toxins you are taking in physically, emotionally, or spiritually. Some drugs and many pesticides produce immediate, dramatic toxic symptoms. Others take a long time to develop into a manifest disease, such as asbestos exposure that invisibly leads to lung cancer. It is no surprise that toxicity diseases such as cardiovascular disease and cancer have increased as our world has become more toxic. Many skin problems, allergies, arthritis, and obesity are others. In addition, a wide range of less frightening symptoms, such as headaches, fatigue, pains, coughs, constipation, gastrointestinal problems, and problems from immune weakness, can all be related to toxicity.

## YOUR BODY IS A TOTAL SYSTEM

You were given five central systems that work together moment by moment to eliminate toxins. It is your responsibility to maintain their health. These systems include the *respiratory*—lungs, bronchial tubes, throat, sinuses, and nose; *gastrointestinal*—liver, gallbladder, colon, and whole GI tract; *urinary*—kidneys, bladder, and urethra; *skin and dermal*—sweat and sebaceous glands and tears; and *lymphatic*—lymph channels and lymph nodes.

The liver, as regards detoxification, filters out foreign substances and wastes from the blood, metabolically altering the toxins and making them easier for the organs to eliminate and less harmful to the body. It also dumps wastes through the bile into the intestines, where much waste is eliminated. The kidneys filter wastes from the blood into the urine, while the lungs remove volatile gases as we breathe. We also clear heavy metals through sweating. Our sinuses and skin may also be accessory elimination organs whereby excess mucus or toxins can be released, as with sinus congestion or skin rashes.

A detoxification program is designed to safely and gently enhance your body's own natural processes. It can be done at several levels and refers to many different programs that cleanse the body of toxins. Anything that promotes elimination can be said to help us detoxify. Drinking more water will usually help you eliminate more toxins. Eating more fruits and vegetables—the high-water-content, cleansing foods—and less meat and dairy products creates less congestion and more elimination. Some programs are directed toward specific organs, such as the liver or kidneys or skin. The secret to great health and feeling great is to combine these detoxification programs into a lifestyle program that works for you. The goal is to become so aware of your body that you know when things are right and instinctively know what you need. It can happen!

Is it possible to go overboard on detoxifying? Certainly, and I see it occasionally. Some people go to extremes with fasting, laxatives, enemas, colonics, diuretics, and exercise, and begin to lose essential nutrients from their body. Some people push it to the point where they experience dangerous protein or vitamin-mineral deficiencies, even becoming paranoid to the extent of bondage! But the vast percentage of our health concerns result from the opposite of going overboard on detoxifying.

It is proven that many common serious and chronic diseases may be diminished or eliminated by a program of cleansing. People with addictions to any substance regularly benefit from detoxification programs, even if it is only the temporary avoidance of the addictive agent or agents. You will feel better when your system gets rid of the unchanged or partially changed toxins that cause negative symptoms. Your immune system will be strengthened in its relentless battle against infections, and you may also reduce the risk of developing cancer. Many of the poisons (toxins) that we take in or make are stored in the fatty tissues. Obesity is almost always associated with toxicity. When we lose weight, we reduce our fat and thereby our toxic load.

## WHAT ARE YOU EATING?

Step #1—start eating right. If you cut your toxic intake, you cut your need for cleansing. I've heard it said that a Twinkie has a shelf life of twenty years. What does that say about the synthetic chemicals that get into our systems? If you don't correct a bad diet, you drastically reduce the effectiveness of any other cleansing methods you use. I have one entire chapter in my book, *How to Feel Great All the Time*, dedicated to my preference in detoxification diets, which is called the Levitical Diet. I favor it because it is well balanced and proven to have been effective for thousands of years.

Detoxification diets help the body eliminate toxins in many ways. They generally eliminate the foods that commonly trigger problems with digestion and elimination. Foods such as wheat and dairy products are often the cause of allergies. Refined, processed, and junk foods are also out for any detoxification program to work. Sugar is drastically cut because of its "empty calories" and tendency to produce hypoglycemia as well as feed cancer cells. Meats are cut back or eliminated because they may contain hormones, antibiotics, and require many enzymes for digestion.

Natural vegetarian diets are cleansing and bring the body several benefits. You get plenty of fiber to stimulate the bowels as well as generous amounts of vitamins to feed and nourish all the eliminative organs. They also include a valuable source of enzymes, since most vegetarian diets are eaten raw. However, even vegetarians can be very off balance due to a lack of good protein and essential salts.

My favorite diet is about 70 percent fruits, vegetables, nuts, and grains; 25 percent cold-water fish and hormone-free chicken; and about 3-5 percent hormone-free red meat.

Once again, by knowing your body, you will know what you need.

Whatever diet you choose, *it must be balanced.* If you have any questions regarding your diet, consult a professional nutritionist, naturopath, or physician.

## WHAT ARE YOU DRINKING?

In another chapter of *How to Feel Great All the Time*, I deal extensively with the importance of water in any type of detoxification program. Your body does not have a better detoxifying friend than water. To adequately help dilute and eliminate toxin accumulations from your body, I recommend that you drink half your body weight in ounces of steam-distilled water every day. From the vital flushing of the kidneys and liver to keeping your skin looking good and feeling soft, the benefits are universal. I suggest you drink water 30-60 minutes before each meal and even at night to help flush toxins during your body's natural elimination time.

## FROM START TO FINISH

While it's a subject most of us prefer not to discuss, cleansing the bowels consistently is a vital key to good health. Your bowels should move like a newborn's, many times a day. One movement now and then is dangerous, but can be changed. When the bowels slow down, the bad news begins. First, there is an increase of bad bacteria in the small intestine and putrefaction in the large intestine. The battle ensues when the bad bacteria weaken your immune system (which is located in the small intestine) and can result in digestive complications. When only partly digested proteins and bacterial toxins cross the intestinal wall, they can cause allergies.

Untreated, it gets ugly. The walls of the bowels become weak and deformed, as with diverticulitis, and hard crusts cover the intestinal walls and restrict movement within the bowels. In severe cases, the products of putrefaction cross the weakened walls of the large intestine and enter the bloodstream. The whole body may become poisoned, and it is possible to seriously damage your body. Enemas and colonics may be needed to break up and cleanse the bowel encrustation.

Reabsorbed toxins are carried back to the liver for recycling and elimination, causing stress to the liver, which then produces extra bile salts that are linked to increased cholesterol levels. Also, when the bowels constipate and toxin levels increase, the bad bacteria grow to outnumber the normal flora and cause dysbiosis. Every part of your nervous system may be affected, and sometimes the heart or brain takes the brunt of the damage.

The easiest way to correct these intestinal problems is a diet of predominately raw foods. A high-quality fiber diet of fresh fruits and vegetables gets the bowels moving and strengthens the bowel walls. You may want to add extra fiber by drinking a glass of water (juice) with psyllium husk powder or another herbal laxative or 1/2 cup of oat bran daily to speed up the process. But it's unwise to become dependent on herbal laxatives. There is no substitute for an excellent fibrous diet to cleanse the bowels as well as bring down bad cholesterol naturally.

## DON'T FORGET THE SKIN

The skin is the largest organ and one of our best eliminative organs of our body. Skin cleansing is therefore a vital part of the detoxification process, particularly when it comes to the heavy metals (aluminum and mercury) that are eliminated through the skin's pores when we sweat. Consistent exercise, steam rooms, and sauna baths are excellent ways to remove toxins from the skin and maximize your health.

Basic skin care is a daily matter, beginning with using natural soaps when you bathe. Skin care products made from chemicals may be cheaper, but remember that those chemicals *will* be absorbed into the bloodstream. Though the amount may be small, it is the cumulative effect of the chemicals that damages your health over the long run. If your body has a toxicity problem, you will notice the difference when you move to natural products on your body. Especially stay away from sodium laurel sulfate—a known carcinogen.

Dry skin brushing is easy to do and helps in removing the outer dead skin layers and keeps the pores open. You will need to buy a natural bristle brush or bath mitt and expect to spend five minutes for brushing your skin. Use light pressure and a circular motion, then shower and moisturize your skin. When detoxifying, the cellular turnover on the skin speeds up, and thus the dead cells coming off will be greater!

Another good technique for cleansing the skin is to towel off roughly until the skin gets slightly red. It will only take you a few minutes more than usual.

Food grade hydrogen peroxide baths are excellent for energy and detoxifying. Epsom salts baths are also very good. For each bath you will need between 8-16 ounces of Epsom salts and 3 ounces of sea salt. Run comfortable warm water and add the salts and dissolve them. Soak for 10-20 minutes and then scrub the skin gently with soap on a natural fiber. Within a few minutes the water will turn murky. The darkness to the water is because of heavy metals coming out of the skin. Get out of the bath carefully, as you may feel light-headed. Then wrap yourself in several towels (you may sweat heavily afterward) and go to bed. Make sure you have water at your bedside because you will be thirsty. Do this once a week during a detoxification program, but once a month is sufficient normally.

Good skin care also requires good nutrition and an abundance of water. Since your skin is mainly fat, you need high-quality fats and oils from natural sources to keep your skin healthy. Olive oil is an excellent source as well as evening primrose and Vitamin E, and combinations of essential fatty acids.

## "FRIENDLY" BACTERIA

A key to improving our digestive functions, the immune system, and overall health is the constant restoration of healthy intestinal flora ("friendly" bacteria). It is such an important part of your detoxification process that I devoted an entire chapter on *"Candida Albicans"* in my book, *How to Feel Great All the Time*. I go into detail on the essential role of the normal flora of our gastrointestinal track to defend our body from the pathogenic species of bacteria and to perform many vital functions, one of which is the detoxification of toxic chemicals. When our normal flora are present, they secrete mediators in which the pathogenic forms cannot grow.

However, antibiotics kill off the good bacteria as well as the bad and allow the bad to repopulate and develop antibiotic resistance. Natural forms of antibiotics are better, since they do not kill off the good bacteria with the bad and do not allow drug resistance to take place. Fresh, raw garlic, for example, has strong antimicrobial power and is more effective against pathogens than most antibiotics today. Herbal antiseptics and antibacterial tonics are far better and less dangerous to our health than antibiotics.

Replacing our natural flora is a good step for preventing disease and keeping our bowels healthy. Eat fresh and raw vegetables, which will help to restore the normal intestinal flora in your body. Eat yogurt (no Aspartame®) daily, as much as possible, with live active cultures that are documented on the label. Natren Probiotics, daily, creates a good terrain for aerobic bacteria (good bacteria) to live and thrive in.

## HERBAL POWER

Detoxification diets are the primary means to cleansing your system, and herbs have been used medicinally for centuries to supplement the cleansing of the blood and tissues or strengthening the function of specific organs. Many herbs have been proven as powerful neutraceutical agents that can support or even cause detoxification. There are hundreds of possible medicinal herbs, and they also provide vitamins, minerals, and enzymes for excellent nutrition. I have a large section on herbs in the "Nature's Prescriptions for Feeling Great" chapter in *How to Feel Great All the Time* that will help direct you in this area. It includes a chart showing herbal alternatives to drugs, essential medicinal herbs, and specific concerns about herbs.

Herbs can be combined together to fortify those specific herbs that aid specific organs. These are found commonly in organic food stores. But it is possible for herbs to interact negatively with one another. If you suspect a bad interaction, consult your physician or pharmacist.

Herbs may be used as teas, salves, tinctures, poultices, capsules, tablets, and concentrated extracts. Always follow the manufacturer's advice regarding the dose. Herbal teas are an easy way to start to enhance your health throughout the day. They are a delicious substitute to break the coffee habit and a potent source of health modulators.

Many people utilize an herbal cleanse. For example, first thing in the morning they may drink a glass of steam-distilled water with a teaspoon of blackstrap molasses and a teaspoon of apple cider vinegar added. During the morning they drink a glass of water with psyllium husk powder, which they follow with a second glass of water. During their meals they take digestive enzymes. Between meals they may take liver herbs and drink herbal teas that specifically help support the liver.

## THE FIGHT AGAINST FREE RADICALS

In the process of metabolism or oxidation, our body cells produce molecules called free radicals. They are unstable molecules that attempt to steal electrons from any available source, such as our body tissues. Antioxidants, such as beta-carotene, Vitamins A, E, and especially C, and selenium, work to neutralize these unstable chemicals and protect us from them. Vitamin C is very essential to any detoxification program because the body uses it for energy to process and eliminate these toxic wastes. The more antioxidants we get in our diets, the more we are able to stop these damaging effects. The main source of antioxidants is fruits, vegetables, nuts, grains, and cold-pressed plant oils.

Antioxidants are essential for detoxification because they help cells neutralize free radicals that can cause mutations and cellular damage. This damage is partly responsible for a wide range of illnesses, including all the degenerative diseases such as arthritis, cardiovascular disease, Alzheimer's, and cancer. Any shortage of antioxidants can become catastrophic to one's health. When our antioxidants are low, energy is not available and detoxification cannot take place in a normal fashion. Therefore, toxins accumulate or are stored until they can be processed.

Other excellent sources of antioxidants are found in bioflavonoids, grape seed extract, ginseng, garlic, molybdenum, DHEA, wheat and barley grass, Echinacea, manganese, carotenoids, Ginkgo Biloba, melatonin, L-Cysteine, acetyl-l-carnite, CoQ10, milk thistle, and B-vitamins.

## YOU ARE WHAT YOU ABSORB

Enzymes have a major impact on your health and detoxification. They help digest and absorb proteins, carbohydrates or starches, lipids or fats. Absorption is absolutely crucial to your health. They also clean up dead tissues, enhance your own enzyme capacity, and help the bowels in cleansing, because they liquefy the bowel content and make for a quicker passage. The quicker the toxins are out of your system, the better your health is, and the better you feel!

While vitamins and minerals get significant attention, don't minimize the role of enzymes. Vitamins and minerals are used to activate enzymes, but enzymes do the hard work of detoxifying toxins and supporting the metabolism of the body.

The best source of enzymes is fresh raw fruits and vegetables, which can be supplemented with multidigestive enzymes. Unfortunately, enzymes are destroyed by processing and cooking. If you eat a high proportion of processed foods, you lose out on these vital ingredients. By eating a wide range of foods, as close to their raw state as possible, you can enjoy all these benefits.

The liver is the source of most detoxification enzymes, which it either makes or stores.

To aid the liver in removing and eliminating wastes and toxins, enzymes are best taken with meals. This way they aid in digestion.

## LIVER CLEANSE

An excellent way to stimulate the liver to detoxify itself is with coffee enemas. We refer to this as a "Liver Cleanse." They are not for the function of cleansing the intestines. This enema is most often used in metabolic cancer therapy and is extremely valuable in many successful detoxification programs. Coffee enemas alkalinize the first part of the intestines, enhance enzyme function, and stimulate the production and release of bile. The coffee is absorbed through the colon wall and travels via the portal vein directly to the liver. When it stimulates the liver to produce bile, it can cause nausea. A little nausea is desirable, but if it is too great, reduce the amount of coffee used or use the enema on a full stomach. The coffee should be stronger than for drinking. Do not dilute the coffee.

The type of coffee to be used is ground (drip) coffee, not instant or decaffeinated. Mix 2 tablespoons of coffee to 1 quart of steam-distilled water. Use 2 cups at body temperature, twice daily. Take this enema preferably on your knees or lie down on your back, legs drawn close to abdomen, and breathe deeply while the enema is given slowly. Retain the fluid for 10 to 15 minutes.

To detoxify the liver in serious conditions, take two coffee enemas per day. Follow this routine for two weeks, then coffee enemas should be reduced to only one per week for one month.

Your body may have a buildup of toxins or poisons from time to time. Symptoms indicating toxicity are a decrease in appetite, headaches, increase in tiredness, and a general lack of well-being. When these occur, increase coffee enemas once again to one per day until symptoms subside or for a maximum of three to four days.

I also recommend a liver dysfunction diet, which is designed to bring healing to the liver. It must contain high-quality protein, such as white turkey meat, leg of lamb, wild game, white low-fat cheese, yogurt, cottage cheese, goat's milk, sprouted seeds and grains, raw nuts (especially almonds), and sesame butter or ground sesame seeds sprinkled over food, raw and steamed vegetables of all kinds.

# Mercury Toxicity

While it is beyond the scope of this booklet to cover the dangers of mercury toxicity related to dental fillings, the fact is that mercury comprises about 50 percent of the most common filling in the world called silver-mercury amalgam. This amalgam also contains copper, tin, silver, and zinc. There are many factors that can increase the release of mercury emissions into your system, but the fact that mercury is released at all is scary. Many experts feel that the amount of mercury released is adequate to contribute significantly to disease processes.

Where does all the mercury go? Into your body. Absorption of mercury occurs the fastest from the area under your tongue and the insides of your cheeks. Being in such close proximity to the fillings, the efficiency of absorption is great. From these tissues, the mercury can destroy adjacent tissues or travel to the lymphatic drainage system and directly into the bloodstream. From the bloodstream, mercury can travel to any cell in the body, where it can either disable or destroy the tissues. Mercury can also travel directly from the fillings into the lungs, where it then enters into the bloodstream, and every cell in the body becomes a potential target.

The ability of mercury to travel throughout the body and its accompanying destruction are what define mercury toxicity. It may favor nerve tissue for a destruction target, but the kidney is high up on its hit list. After these two areas, it can wreak havoc in any tissue that gets in its way. It can alter almost anything in the body; therefore, mercury should not be allowed to enter for any reason.

This is especially problematic if someone has a tooth or teeth that have leached a significant amount of mercury into the body. Detoxification will not help to any great extent until the mercury is taken out. Many doctors will not even do chelation or treat new patients until the mercury is eliminated or the entire tooth is removed.

## THE HEALING CRISIS

In the fasting section, I address this more fully because of the intensity of fasting's detoxification process. Nevertheless, even during milder detoxification programs, it is possible for your body to detoxify too rapidly and have toxins released faster than the body can eliminate them. When this occurs, you may suffer from headaches, nausea, vomiting, depression, and even old aches and pains you forgot you had! This is a good thing! It means your body is working. If this occurs, back off the program and proceed at a slower pace. Forcing a detoxification process too quickly can have negative results.

According to naturopathic theory, any symptoms of the disease that have previously been experienced may also be experienced transiently during detoxification, and I have seen this occur quite often. However, sometimes it's difficult to know what is going on inside. Should you treat the problems that come up or simply watch them? Since my basic approach is to allow the body to heal itself and support the natural healing process whenever possible, that is what I try to do unless it becomes intolerable.

For many of us, especially the new or inexperienced, it is wise to begin any special program, diet, or lifestyle changes with a few days at home or possibly over a weekend. In time, experience will tell you what is best. Most of us can maintain a regular work schedule during a cleanse or detoxification program (you'll probably feel great), but it may be easier to begin a program on a Friday, as the first few days are usually the hardest.

# FASTING

**FASTING IS A PERIOD** OF RESTRICTED food intake that detoxifies the body, giving the organs a rest and bringing natural healing by cleansing the body. But fasting is not only excellent for the body, it is also breath to the spirit as well. God says in Isaiah 58 that He has a chosen fast that is redemptive for every area of your life. Your spirit, mind, and body are included so that no disease will come upon you! Fasting facilitates this divine freedom. "Then your light will break forth like the dawn, and your healing will quickly appear." Your fast can be a time to be restored to a right relationship with Him! He will go before you as your righteousness, and His glory will be your guardian.

What a marvelous incentive to begin a fast! Blessings to all who choose to make this exciting healing journey! May your health spring forth speedily. God will be with you!

Fasting has been practiced for centuries

among many societies, particularly for religious purposes. Among the Jews, the Day of Atonement was the most prominent occasion for a public fast (Leviticus 16:29-31; 23:27-36; Numbers 29:7). The Old Testament also refers to many special fasts, both public and individual (Judges 20:26; 1 Samuel 14:24; 31:13; 2 Samuel 1:12; 12:16-23; 1 Kings 21:27; 2 Chronicles 20:3). Jesus Christ was led by the Spirit to a forty day and night fast in the desert, which was followed by a time of intense temptation (Matthew 4:1-11). He gave His followers instructions for how He wanted them to fast (Matthew 6:16-18), and there is clear evidence of fasting in the early church (Acts 13:2-3; 14:23).

## WHAT ARE THE BENEFITS?

I have seen in my fasting and *Candida* clinic that fasting is both a primary means of detoxifying the body, shedding unwanted pounds, and a wonderful aid to spiritual renewal. While our emphasis for purposes of feeling great focuses on the cleansing of the body and weight loss, keep in mind that the health of your spiritual life is intrinsic to your overall health. There is no substitute for experiencing on a daily basis the fullness of joy from being in a right relationship with God.

Fasting has been proven to be the most effective means of getting the body into a natural healing process. It is also an instrument to literally reset the body's odometer and help reverse the aging process. Disease and aging begin when the normal process of cell regeneration and rebuilding slows down. This slowdown is caused by the accumulation of waste products in the tissues, which interferes with the nourishment and oxygenation of cells. This may happen at any age, and when it occurs, the cells' resistance to disease diminishes and various ills start to appear. Given the fact that at any given moment one-fourth of all our cells are dead and in replacement, it is of vital importance that the dying cells are decomposed and eliminated from the system as efficiently as possible. Quick and effective elimination of dead cells stimulates the building and growth of new cells.

Hippocrates (c. 460-377 B.C.), the Greek physician often called "the father of medicine," spoke of this well over two thousand years ago. He said, "Food should be our medicine, and medicine should be our food, but to eat when you are sick is to feed your illness." Such ancient advice contains true wisdom. When you stop eating, your organs rest, and all the energy in your body is directed to healing.

By ridding the body of toxicity, you will find yourself more alert and energetic, requiring less sleep, and you will experience a keener sense of awareness to those around you as well as to your own spirit and the Holy Spirit. In simple words, you will find yourself being led by your spirit and not by your appetite.

In Germany, Dr. Otto Buchinger Jr., who is an authority on fasting, has supervised over 90,000 successful fasting and detox programs and has used these methods to treat virtually every disease—rheumatic conditions, digestive disorders, skin conditions, cardiovascular disorders, and more. Diminished hormone levels can be restored simply by cleansing the body.

We now know that by fasting only three days a month, you can increase your life-span by five to seven years. An interesting study was conducted in Europe with centenarians (those living to be over one hundred years of age). The study showed that there was only one common link among this age group—they all ate less than the average person, and they fasted often! Cornell University studies have shown that by keeping animals from overeating and implementing systematic fasting, their lives can be increased up to 50 percent.

Another study, called "The Hunger Treatment," was conducted in Russia in 1986 at a hospital for the mentally ill. The study lasted for sixty days and involved eight hundred schizophrenics who were made to partake in a juice fast. After only 25-30 days of cleansing, 64 percent of the patients improved mentally, which led to the assessment that two-thirds of the patients diagnosed with mental problems were actually in such a state of toxicity that the brain could not function properly. Since that study we know that many misdiagnosed mental illnesses can be attributed to heavy metal poisoning as well as a lack of nutrients. By giving the patient the right nutrients, balance can occur and health be restored.

## HOW FASTING WORKS

Fasting means to not eat, but it doesn't mean you should restrict yourself to water only. In fact, juice fasting has proven to be the most effective way to restore your health back to the way God intended.

During a prolonged fast (after the first three days), your body will live on its own substance. When it is deprived of needed nutrition, particularly of proteins and fats, it will burn and digest its own tissues by the process of *autolysis,* or self-digestion. But your body will not do this indiscriminately! Through the divine wisdom of our Great Creator, your body will first decompose and burn those cells and tissues that are diseased, damaged, aged, or dead. In the fasting process, your body feeds itself on the most impure and inferior materials, such as dead cells and morbid accumulations—tumors, abscesses, fat deposits, etc. Dr. Buchinger says, "Fasting is a refuse disposal, a burning of rubbish." The essential body tissues and vital organs, the glands, the nervous system, and the brain are not damaged or digested in a fast.

In general, three- to ten-day fasts are recommended for health and longevity. The body needs three to five days of fasting to actually begin the autolysis process whereby the body attacks inferior matter in the body and begins the healing process. A five-day fast essentially clears debris before disease gets started. A ten-day fast works to attack disease that has already begun and often eliminates problems from the body before the symptoms arise. During the fast, the function of the eliminative organs—liver, kidneys, lungs, and the skin—is greatly increased, and accumulated toxins and waste are quickly expelled. During the fast, toxins in the urine can be ten times higher than normal.

## HOW TO FAST

If you have never fasted before, it is best to start with several one-day fasts before moving on to a three-day fast. Do these once a week until you feel comfortable moving on.

Then have a three-day fast once a month. As a preparation for it, reduce the amount of food and eat only whole raw organic foods two to three days before you begin your fast. I recommend beginning the fast on a Friday evening and extending it through Monday evening. Most people are at home on weekends and can easily do their juicing and cleansing with few interruptions. For many people the second day feels the worst, so it's best to have that on a day of rest. Think of it as a time to give your body a rest, to let it retune itself, and to aid in its healing process.

Start each day of your fast with room temperature steam-distilled water. Every day you should be drinking half of your body weight in ounces of water. For example, if you weigh 150 pounds, drink 75 ounces of water each day. Health science consensus currently believes that steam-distilled water is the best for fasting as well as daily use. Steam-distilled water is the only water that actually goes in and pulls out toxins from the organs. It literally pulls out the mire that gets caught in the follicles of the colon and breeds disease. You will also find that steam-distilled water helps curb your appetite, unlike drinks or juice that causes your body to want more.

The best juices are the ones you juice yourself. Fresh organic veggies are in supply at your local health food store as well as grocery stores. Stock up on the freshest you can find. During a fast, my favorite juice is a carrot, beet, and ginger combination. Feel free to use a variety of veggies and fruits. Fresh lemon, cabbage, beet, carrot, grape (including the seeds), apple (skin and seeds), green combos made from leafy greens such as spinach, kale, turnips, etc.—these are all excellent detoxifiers.

Raw cabbage juice is known to aid in the recovery from ulcers, cancer, and all colon problems. However, it must be fresh, not stored. Cabbage loses its Vitamin U content after sitting for only a short time.

Another excellent juice blend is three carrots, two stalks of celery, one turnip, two beets, a half head of cabbage, a quarter bunch of parsley, and a clove of garlic. This could be one of the best juices on our planet for the restoration of the body from many ailments.

Another favorite juice preparation is Stanley Borroughs's "Master Cleanser." In a gallon of steam-distilled water, mix the juice of five fresh lemons and a half cup of grade B maple syrup. Add one or more tablespoons of hot cayenne pepper (at least 90,000 heat units) to your taste tolerance. This is especially good for alkalinizing the body and raising body temperature to help resolve infection and flu-type illnesses.

Pure vegetable broths with no seasonings added are also good. To prepare these, gently boil vegetables, including lots of onions and garlic, for 30 minutes. Do not eat the stew, but strain the broth and drink the juice two or three times a day.

The juices, broths, and water will keep you adequately full as well as provide you with more nutrients than most people normally get from their diets. If you must eat something, have a slice of watermelon. Organic grapes with seeds are also good, especially Concord grapes, which have a powerful antioxidant effect. Alternatively, fresh applesauce made with the skins on and the seeds intact, processed in a blender or food processor, is satisfying and won't significantly disrupt your fast.

A great way to top off your day, whether fasting or not, is to have a half cup of oat bran with a non-dairy milk (soy, almond, or rice). This helps to cleanse the colon by adding fiber and has been shown to cut the risk of cancer by 30 percent! I have found that eating oat bran before going to bed suits my body well and seems to aid in a peaceful night's rest.

Green drinks can also be an added bonus to

any fast. We have created one called *Creation's Bounty*, which is a whole raw organic food with all the nutrients your body needs. There may also be other green drinks to choose from at your local health food store.

## DAILY SUGGESTED PROTOCOL FOR YOUR FAST

Start with 4-8 ounces of *Clustered Water*™. This will help to clean the lymphatic system.

Fifteen minutes later take 1-2 ounces of *Body Oxygen*™.

Thirty to forty minutes later have a green drink.

Prepare your favorite fresh juice combination, which you can alternate with Stanley Burroughs's lemonade drink.

If you don't have a juicer, use the best organic juice from your grocery store.

Prepare fresh vegetables broth to sip in between juices and/or green smoothies.

Remember to drink as much steam-distilled water as possible.

A good liquid mineral supplement will aid in rapid healing.

If you must eat, remember—grapes, watermelon, or fresh applesauce.

Rest whenever you feel weak during a fast. Deep-breathing exercises and frequent showers are helpful.

## FASTING DON'TS

■ Don't fast on water alone!

■ Don't chew gum or mints. This starts the digestive juices flowing and is harmful to the system. When your stomach releases hydrochloric acid in the gut, but nothing ever gets down there, is it a surprise that you have a stomachache?

Don't drink orange or tomato juice on a fast. They are too acidic.

Don't ever eat junk foods, especially before the fast. The last food you eat will be the next food you crave. If you eat junk food, you'll want more of it. If you eat veggies, you'll want something healthy. Our bodies are designed by God to want healthy food, but when we eat the wrong things, we deaden our senses to what is good. Did you ever notice when you eat a fast-food burger you feel full for about 30 minutes, and then suddenly you're hungry again! This is because your body is so desperate for nutrition it is still trying to get you to eat something it can actually benefit from instead of dead, unbeneficial calories?

## EXTENDED FASTS

There are fasts that last up to 100 days. Twenty-, thirty-, and forty-day fasts are common to individuals with extraordinary needs. These fasts must be scientifically supervised, though, and not just undertaken at will. Proper liquid nutrition must be ingested, and additional supplementation may be required. Your program must be tailor-made for you and your personal makeup. For individuals with these needs, such as extreme obesity, disease, etc., I recommend that you contact a specialist that is listed in the back of my book, *How to Feel Great All the Time*, or call my office at 817-236-8557.

## WHILE YOU FAST

When going on a juice fast of three days or longer, some experts advise taking an herbal laxative on the first day of the fast and every two or three days during a longer fast. I prefer and personally recommend enemas during a fast as an absolute must. Enemas assist the body in its detoxifying effort by cleansing out all the toxic waste from the alimentary canal. A healthy, normal adult is carrying around 7-14 pounds of waste (that's the weight of a newborn baby!). Think of what an immune-compromised or overweight person may have stored up. People continually ask me why they are still having large bowel movements after several days of not eating. The answer is simple—most people have years of backup to clean out.

Enemas should be taken at least once, preferably twice, a day during your fast—one after rising in the morning and the other before going to bed. One pint to one quart of lukewarm distilled water is sufficient. Enema bags are available in any drugstore. One word of medical caution—enemas tend to delete the potassium level, therefore care must be taken for proper supplementation.

Although naturopaths have used both enemas and colonic irrigation for many years in their detoxification methods, its use is not without controversy. Fiber supplements are now available that can be taken by mouth and achieve similar purposes.

## MAINTENANCE AFTER A FAST

Fasting brings the body back to doing what it is designed to do, which is for you to accomplish the will of God without the hindrances of fatigue, obesity, and illness. Most people, following initial withdrawal from chemical dependencies (including caffeine and sugar), dramatically see and feel a difference in their health status by day three of a good fast. People commonly feel lighter and more energized and notice improvements in complexion and eye color. These changes indicate you are on your way back to optimal health.

Always break the fast gently. Whole raw organic foods may be used. Nothing heavy or chemical laden should be eaten, such as processed foods. For powerful aid in rebuilding the immune system before and after the fast, drink Pau d'arco and Echinacea tea mixed with one-third unsweetened cranberry juice four times a day.

Lightly steamed vegetables in their broth with whole grain brown rice can be added slowly and used as part of a maintenance diet.

## DEALING WITH THE HEALING CRISIS

When you alter your diet, especially during a fast, changes occur that are often misunderstood. Far too often I have seen individuals who were properly detoxing, cleansing, and healing quit just before the finish line. This is simply due to misunderstanding the way the body was designed by God to heal itself. The following will hopefully give you clarity as to what to expect when you are in the eliminative process that brings healing. Remember, the Word says, "At the proper time we will reap a harvest if we do not give up" (Galatians 6:9).

Dr. Bernard Jensen has defined a healing crisis as "an acute reaction resulting from the ascendance of the natural healing forces over disease conditions. Its tendency is toward recovery, and it is, therefore, in conformity with the natural reconstruction principle put innately in us by God." It is the direct result of an industrious effort of every organ in the body to eliminate waste products and set the stage for regeneration. Through this constructive process toward health, old tissues are replaced with new.

In a healing crisis there is usually a fever, which shows that the body is fighting to burn out residues of old viruses, bacteria, and disease in general. Symptoms of the healing crisis may at first be identical to the disease it is meant to heal. But the real distinction is elimination. Elimination is usually significantly increased, due to the fact that all the eliminative organs are doing their part to rid the body of harmful toxins and buildup. This is just the opposite in a diseased state, when the body is usually either constipated or very irregular, leaving the body in an unsatisfactory condition and compounding the trouble. When elimination occurs, you know that the body is in a purifying and cleansing process.

In time the new tissue becomes strong enough to take its place in the various activities of the body. The old tissue is expelled through various means—phlegm, mucous, sweat, bowels, etc. As the process of building up new cellular structure has been accomplished, the real healing is taking place.

According to Dr. Jensen, there are three stages to the healing crisis:

■ Eliminative—the body ridding itself of debris.

■ Transitional—new tissue is maturing.

■ Building—the body is then going into homeostasis, a state of health, the way God intended us to live.

A healing crisis usually lasts about three days. During that time, various aches, pains, and symptoms of ailments from long ago seem to rear their ugly head. Some people only experience a slight headache, while others may feel as if they are on their last leg. All of this is dependent upon the degree of cleansing the body needs to accomplish. If the crisis is bearable, work through it, as the rewards are well worth it. If it is unbearable, back off slightly, then try again later. The body will order each step of the crisis from the inside out and from the head down, which is why it usually starts with a headache.

Please keep in mind that the majority of physical problems the average American is facing is brought on by a poor diet, lack of exercise, and a fast-pace stressful lifestyle. Fasting and detoxing assist in ridding the body of the lifestyle buildups that eventually develop into chronic diseases. One healing crisis may not be enough for complete restoration. You may require a number of cycles of healing crises. Think of it as peeling the layers off an onion.

Keep in mind that the crisis is necessary in order for true healing to take place. You must get rid of the old to bring in the new. Just think of the whole body getting into action to correct ailing organs, joints, and various conditions in the body. True healing can never occur without a real cleansing of the eliminative organs.

After the healing crisis has occurred, strength, energy, and health begin to build. After a cleanse, a healthy diet, proper amounts of oxygen, good water and lots of it, along with a moderate exercise program, you will be giving your body what it needs to stay on track.

As always, you may want to consult your physician regarding any concerns you have about symptoms during what you perceive to be a healing crisis. It is easy to mistake serious medical symptoms for minor symptoms. And always check with your physician before beginning any new cleansing or exercise program.

# VALERIE SAXION'S SILVER CREEK LABS

**THROUGHOUT THIS BOOKLET,** I HAVE noted four products that will aid you in your detoxification efforts as well as promote a healthy body. To order these products or to contact Silver Creek Laboratories for a complete catalog and order form of other nutritional supplements and health products, call (817) 236-8557, or fax (817) 236-5411, or write us at:

7000 Lake Country Dr.
Fort Worth, TX 76179

Body Oxygen. A pleasant-tasting nutritional supplement that is meticulously manufactured with cold pressed aloe vera. The aloe is used as a stabilized carrier for numerous nutritional constituents, including magnesium peroxide and pure anaerocidal oxygen, hawthorne berry, ginkgo biloba, ginseng, and St. John's Wort. It helps naturally fight infections, inflammation, and degeneration by taking oxygen in at the cellular level. It also commonly helps in colon cleansing, regular elimination, and provides a feeling of increased energy and mental alertness.

Candida Cleanse. A decade in coming, this is the most powerful natural agent I know of in the fight against *Candida*. It is specifically formulated for TOTAL *Candida* cleansing. A two-part system is also available to rid the body of *Candida* and parasites called *ParaCease*.

Dr. Lorenzen's Clustered Water is probably the greatest breakthrough in health science product development in this century. Clustered Water, produced at home using one ounce of solution to one gallon of steam-distilled water, replenishes the most vital support for all cellular DNA and the 4,000 plus enzymes that are involved in every metabolic process in your body. This amazing product increases nutrient absorption by up to 600 percent, which means your vitamins and organic foods will deliver far more vital nutrients to your body. It replicates the powerful healing waters of the earth! Excellent for cleaning out lymphatic fluids! It comes in a C-400 formula for those who are generally healthy and detoxed, and a SBX formula for the immune-compromised.

Creation's Bounty. Simply the best, pleasant-tasting, green, whole, raw, organic food supplement available—a blend of whole, raw, organic herbs and grains, principally amaranth, brown rice, spirulina, and flaxseed. This combination of live foods with live enzymes assists your body in the digestion of foods void of enzymes. You will gain vital nutrients, protein, carbohydrates, and good fats to nourish your body and brain, resulting in extra energy and an immunity boost as well. It is a whole food, setting it apart from other green foods on the market.

# Unleash Your Greatness

## AT BRONZE BOW PUBLISHING WE ARE COMMITTED to helping you achieve your **ultimate potential** in functional athletic strength, fitness, natural muscular development, and all-around superb health and youthfulness.

**O**ur books, videos, newsletters, Web sites, and training seminars will bring you the very latest in scientifically validated information that has been carefully extracted and compiled from leading scientific, medical, health, nutritional, and fitness journals worldwide.

**Our goal is to empower you!** To arm you with the best possible knowledge in all facets of strength and personal development so that you can make the right choices that are appropriate for *you*.

Now, as always, **the difference between greatness and mediocrity** begins with a choice. It is said that knowledge is power. But that statement is a half truth. Knowledge is power only when it has been tested, proven, and applied to your life. At that point knowledge becomes wisdom, and in wisdom there truly is *power*. The power to help you choose wisely.

**So join us** as we bring you the finest in health-building information and natural strength-training strategies to help you reach your ultimate potential.